What May Be Lost

5/1/14

For Bob

love

Coy

Cayuga Lake Books

Ithaca, New York

What May Be Lost

by Cory Brown

2014

First printing—January 2014

ISBN: 978-1-60047-942-7

Printed in the USA

0   1   2   3   4   5

What May Be Lost

poems
by

Cory Brown

Table of Contents

Section 1.

Section 2.

Section 3.

Section 4

Section 1.

Monkey in the Tree

I'm in my own tree-house on my second story porch, the hanging plant drooping its hair down in the humidity. I water it daily or it turns ninety-years-old overnight and that's too much of a mirror for me to face. The Jade below it is another story—she's had perky breasts now for several years. My dog snoozing beside me is getting up there in dog years, but can keep up with me still on my jaunts around the block. What I was just a few years ago is difficult to fathom. My life is like a pipe cleaner that for the first time you understand isn't just for twisting into little shapes. Everything justifies its own existence to me these days, the smell of gasoline at the pump, the over-ripe peach in the bowl in front of me, offering itself to my hand on this summer afternoon, like a cloud that shapes itself into a June bug or a bunny. They will both crawl or hop away and I, staring at the sky from my porch, know that, which is how I know to love them.

Bats

From my back porch yesterday at dusk I watched them flicker about
in the near dark, up and down between the tall trees, like peripheral
glimpses of something in a dream, a nightmare even, except I was
watching them straight on. And today, after a long night of tossing and
turning like a bass thrown up on the shore, the hook secure in my thick
wiry lip, I heard in my head that maybe anxiety is my home, that if I
could make my peace with it I could sink down in its cushions, light
up a pipe even, take periodic mid-afternoon naps in its soft folds. I can
see from where I am on the porch again today twin white butterflies
swimming above the garden, the sun lighting them up. There one circles
the tomato plant climbing its round wire trellis next to the overgrown
collards. Should every single thing be accepted into as much light as
it will take, as Ammons says? The kindling beneath Joan of Arc? Job's
locusts and boils? Blossoming hemangiomas? Post-mortem putrescence
and the scars of the Guantanamo tortured? A squirrel's been making a
mockery of the bird feeder all summer long, climbing down from the
roof and scattering seeds onto the garbage cans below. I sometimes watch
him at work, my broom handle in hand, he and I eyeing one another.

Not Yet

It's that dreamlike season again between summer and fall, not yet fall, the old grumpy bus driver who tells you to sit down he'll get you to where you're going don't panic on him. Not yet fall, where we can see from the middle of the tracks standing as if stuck in concrete the oncoming locomotion, as all around us the little omens of debris fall about our heads. In my mind they are all poems, about winning touchdowns on cool nights in Minnesota or Kansas, about the second and third kisses of 14-year-olds that never later, in young- or mid-adulthood, live up to their full-lipped erotic promise. They are about the childhood dog under your bed you thought was just sleeping. They are about difficult births. They are about falling leaves, which makes them about themselves, and two of them slide down on air into one another like two cars moving into the same lane, whose collision becomes a metaphor for the two seasons, or for two lovers: one in an updraft she'd been caught in since childhood when her father would slap her cheek at the dinner table and the other, he, still arcing down as if he's in a swing, the stem of his little-boy-legs out in front of him until he reaches that high moment of suspense when the torso leans back in childlike oblivion, the way his mother, in his mind, tossed herself off that bridge, backwards. No, not yet fall. But the light's at a different slant, a different attitude, shadows longer, and inside the heat is a touch of something threatening itself, felt beneath the skin, a foreshadowing of sorts, of cool nights and of that long sleep from whose depths no one emerges groggy or rested.

Mid-September

The wind stirs the autumn leaves today, or is it the leaves the wind?
Perhaps both are subject to a common force, as if a giant invisible hand
were mixing sugar into warm milk with a giant invisible spoon. And
who am I in the midst of this sweet concoction sipping on air in the late
afternoon's blue light? The light will move on of course, as these leaves
will. Fast-moving leviathan clouds will roll in, or another hour will pass
and another and the house shadow will have crawled away like a lazy
spider. Or like an old actor in a gangster movie—Cagney with a bullet in
his chest—dragging himself around to stretch out the scene. But for now
the light warms my skin, my children half-grown and mostly independent.
I can sit in my yard on an afternoon like this, home early from work, fuss
with the garden and watch my new puppy snap at cornflowers, watch the
bees slurp on okra blooms. And though the maple leaves fall when a gust
forces its way through, they are still green.

A good friend after many years of devotion to his wife lost her to
someone else recently—that's a pain I felt not too long ago. And though
I believe he was less deserving of his loss than I of mine, his wife, from
what he's told me, would disagree. Which goes to show that fidelity
and devotion are no guarantee of marital bliss, and if they aren't, what
is? Those open-wound days of mine are gone now, yet I won't say I'm
happy, for your sake, reader. For you, that would be like watching crabs
copulate—they do it twenty-four hours at a time, one atop the other in
their cold armor; we can't believe what we're seeing and it's boring at
the same time. Besides, happiness is fragile as a spider's web, safe as a
fat New England turkey in mid-November, secure as the back-hair of an
Alaskan Malamute hiking some tropical countryside. Happiness grows
merely to molt, light as feathers.

What May Be Lost

"Your life is first of all what may be lost, its ultimate end to not end."
C. K. Williams

This is what we must work our whole lives to reverse—not to step in front of a bus, but to imagine ourselves discarded as a pulled weed, a dropped-to-the-ground wren, its neck laid out flat from some natural process, the eyes, where the ants are, already gone, the feathers heeding nothing but the commands of a small breeze. We must take that image in, feed it, tuck it in and kiss it goodnight, lie down with it to help it fall asleep—roll quietly out, ease ourselves up so as not to wake it, and when we retire to our own beds not forget our precious guest who, like our own child, lies asleep in the next room. We must relish seeing its sleepy eyes in the morning.

Pattern

Sometimes I see a pattern in my dog's hair resembling a school of fish or the flow of blood, or I see colors on the water's surface in a slow-moving creek. And stacks of books in my bedroom rise and fall, I notice, like the uplift and erosion of a mountain range. And they're all there. That period I just typed is there, and there are more to come. The rain outside and the bedspread on my bed, its floral pattern—there's that word again, that's a pattern itself. But what of patterns of the heart? the romantic type, the cold fish, the sentimentalist, the nihilist who cries at the movies when the alien dies of a mysterious disease that saves all the humans, tears welling up in his eyes that he knows will be worm food soon after his heart stops. Meanwhile he fantasizes about making his life, he thinks, more meaningful, assuming among the autumn leaves the role of a single leaf, with prominent veins and its own array of colors, orange and purple perhaps, a hint of fuchsia, floating down in falling arcs regulated by the laws of nature, from an oak or maple growing in a single season in a single year among a series of seasons and years. But what could all this meaning mean? When he's alone with his music he still cries sometimes, not a painful cry, just a conditioned response: replace the strings with jazz or tough blues and the tears turn to laughter, or indifference. Does consciousness itself impose patterns and thus meaning, such that nihilism is no more possible than being in two places at once, affirmation no more remarkable than the asking of a question, the thinking of a thought?

Realization

When we're young we have no mechanism by which to know ourselves—it's only in the repetition of our behaviors over a span of years that we're allowed a glimpse into the inner sanctum of our identities. It's as if we're under water our entire young adult lives and someone descends from above—a therapist or new lover—not necessarily for your benefit but there they are nonetheless, speaking in a chair in front of you or in your bed resting from a carnival ride of lust—and suddenly they offer an insight about you that makes you gasp. Then they disappear like some genie sucked back into his bottle for another ten thousand years. It's as if they had tapped you on the shoulder and pointed up to reveal a new form of being, the bubbles of your old existence still leaking from your mouth as you respond, "But how will I live without the bubbles?" Then you stand up. You unbend your knees and find yourself in air, a canopy of blue above, clouds you had only dimly perceived through water now drifting in a clarity unimagined before, like lazy gods plump from the self-indulgence immortality affords, propped up on elbows and tossing grapes into one another's mouths with the insouciance of, say, an old fisherman tossing into the bay a sea bass the size of his hand. Their lips stained purple from the grapes, they sip champagne and tell stories about boys with wings falling from the sky, or animal-headed men daring one another to eat a child whole, or they debate the proper fate of a hero or heroine long lost to the depths of the underworld. That would be you of course, and as you're breathing in this new element you realize you can still feel the tap on your shoulder—the melody recently heard—but when you turn to see who's there no one is beside you, not your brother nor sister nor father, all dead now, nor your old friend who charmed you with his late-night guitar playing and who you sometimes miss with a strength akin to hate. That tap may come again, perhaps sooner than you expect. Of course you know who it is this time. You weave through the crowd like a swallow rounding trees, desperate for a glimpse of yourself.

Beyond

The storm shakes the windows in the early morning hours of this cold day. It is January and I am alone, sitting up in bed. My dog is under the covers at my feet, and I am considering aloneness. "As soon as truth is a limit or has limits, its own," writes the philosopher, "and assuming it knows some limits, as the expression goes, truth would be a certain relation to what terminates or determines it." It wouldn't be true to say that I am alone, though no one else is in the house. I cannot go beyond the boundary of my community to say that I am not a part of it. Does my dog at my feet consider herself alone? Meaning keeps me company, if I mean it to. It is a trail I make by making it, walking it and clearing the path, like deer or goats or wild dogs. But perhaps it is not beyond the stretch of the imagination, as the phrase goes, to go beyond meaning in this matter. The history of human migration is full of stories of crossing boundaries beyond the known. Iceland, Greenland, The Bering Strait, and down south The Pitcairns and Easter Island. And right here in upstate New York is one of those destinations. What did borders mean to those early explorers? I hear the train across town whistling along the tracks I walked across a couple of days ago, exploring a new path to the park. I'm sure my daughter meant to call me back, I remember thinking as I walked along the path. And then, getting closer to the lake, I came across a possum and watched its hands scurry it away. Sometimes in this old house I hear the pattering of animal feet in the attic, when the wind shakes the house or when the heat comes on. Ah, I think to myself, it is not my meaning that measures out their winter meals, or times their heart rates—it is not my meaning that counts me as one in this house.

To a Son Leaving Home

You were too young to remember the big yellow house we lived in with
two wells that in summer would both go dry. Out back was an apple
orchard and in the yard was a large black walnut tree and our garden
with zinnias and sweet peas. The house overlooked Cayuga Lake and
one day I strapped you in and took a long drive along the lakeside
slopes, with its fields of grapevines strung on trellises like low-hanging
clotheslines. It was spring or early summer, when the vines are no longer
covered with snow, and I looked at them with their stray tendrils hanging
down and thought they looked like the arms of the thieves that hung
beside Christ, or like those of Christ himself in replicate sacrificing
himself row after row. Most days, though, you and I would stay home.
I would sit at the breakfast table and write and you would play at my feet.
I might watch the steam rise from my coffee cup and arrange the lines
on the page to mimic it. Or I might watch you push your trains back
and forth along the floor and think how you were like me scribbling back
and forth, or I like you. And I could imagine in the poem my coffee cup
on the floor as your steam engine, with little cars behind it hitched to its
handle and you, suddenly small as a mouse and your little engineer cap
pulled down over your ears, leaning back inside the C of the handle and
waving goodbye to me.

Crab Cakes and Corn

We had work to do yesterday but it got up into the 80s so we headed over to the lake with our bagged picnic lunch: crab cakes from the fish guy that drives down from Boston once a week and corn from who knows where, it being April and all. In the 80s in late April—glorious! But it was the kind of day that makes you worry in your pleasure, what with climate change and all. I was bending over the sink today brushing my teeth, and my nose starts bleeding for no apparent reason—I'm always tired and my eyes are often red and itchy. To make myself feel better I like to roll a ball point pen across this paper my wife bought me, a tablet of newsprint that goes wider than most, and the paper resembles the kind in those big chief tablets we used to get in grade school, with that rough recycled feel that makes it a pleasure to roll the pen across—I would say "glide," which might convey the feeling more poetically, but "roll" has the virtue of being literally accurate. But rolling the pen's ball across this paper is not as pleasurable as rolling it across the surface of an eraser or a rubber ball—a pleasure by the way I heard referred to by a New Yorker essayist as having never before been mentioned in print (well, here it is a second time). It's hard to find those materials—erasers or rubber balls—in as wide a form as this paper, so this paper does the trick for now. It's the kind of pleasure that reminds me of bicycling. I sometimes think the bicycle must be the one modern gift from God, practically proof of His existence, given as recompense I suppose for the submachine gun, howitzers, tear gas, napalm, and of course herpes. I mean, the way you can propel along quietly on a street with the slightest effort and gaze around you at the pretty little houses while a breeze tickles your eyelashes and cools the back of your neck. Imagine yourself injured in the thigh or ankle or foot, severe enough to disable you for a while and then you get better and go out bicycling on a beautiful spring day. Be prepared for a pleasure that may stun you. And because your injury keeps it from being an effortless exertion, you won't take it for granted. That's what happens sometimes when you come close to losing something. I'm often choking myself on Spanish peanuts, not intentionally of course, but I'll come away from the experience, which sometimes lasts as long as several seconds, with a new appreciation for breath and life. I would say try it sometime, but that would be a silly suggestion.

Life

Funny how the gray-blue sky today, early May, seems to cling to my sleeve—I can't shake it, fused in my mind with the sweet smell of honeysuckle and lilac. I was walking the dog the other day and found myself swimming in it, its blossoms everywhere, like music—and felt I was strolling through a nudist colony, all that fragrant vulnerability just asking to be swatted or pinched, and it occurred to me life is so painful it's a puncture wound that never heals, and stays with you for eternity. I don't know what that word means, though—eternity. I've been hearing Emily Dickinson use it for years, but I think we've lost the capacity to conceive of capaciousness on that level. Who's to say we would even want it, not leaving us much time to experience the everydayness of a rush hour, all that genuine rage. But what is time anyway but a whistling tune we can hear down the hall of our lives, yes, but hardly be in, as if it were something you could dive into and swim through. No, time is more like a taste, a ripe mango on a bed of rice, sautéed with raisins and walnuts and olives and sometimes you bite down hard on a pit, or eat too much of it and it comes back up on you, say, the next morning when you least expect it. But I'll put on my glasses anyway, as if it's any other morning, and listen all day to that sweet Doppler effect.

There I Might Live

I would like not to abide by a faith in motion for its own sake. I would like to live sitting still, my back yard as exotic a landscape as there is, sycamores, maples, and birch my wildebeests and Bengal tigers. "Wherever I sat, there I might live," wrote Thoreau, "and the landscape radiated from me accordingly." But aren't we always in motion? Walden Pond today is not Thoreau's. His no longer exists and never did you could say, given time's hyper-fleeting character, which brings us to the sticky debate between time and existence. O would that they would stick! That there would be at least sometimes something more than debate, more than "is life mere consciousness?" I am propped up in bed this morning, the summer fan moving air for my comfort, the computer glowing. Is what I'm sensing all idea? When my lover returns today or tomorrow and I find her breasts in my hands cupped, will they be mere thoughts? Will her lips on mine, then her nipple in my mouth, be the mere thinking of lips on lips, nipple in mouth? Will my devotion and hers be the stuff of pure unstuff? Can there be nothing but the asking?

Current

There's a way in which pop songs are like small streams winding their
way through your head day in day out. And sometimes late at night
they flood. I'm lying here with the radio on, my TV in the next room is
a log floating downstream, my dining room table one of those islands
in the middle we build bridges to if the river is narrow enough. I'll say
it's a grassy island that birds land on, on their way north or south, my
feet scuffling across the floor like fish. I think I'm one of those fish that
stays in one place as the current rushes past. Each day without touching
someone is cloudless but snowy, big globs of it floating down to silence
the doubters. Doubt is the squirrel that haunts my dreams, or the monkey
I saw once on the streets of New Delhi, who came right up to the cab
and looked at me as if she expected to be crowned queen for the day.
I never tell anyone of the earthquakes I've been daydreaming about, like
the little one I felt on that island in Greece. I was sitting on the steps of a
bank looking at your mouth in the clouds and it was reminding me of a
dream I'd once had, in which I stood staring at an image floating across
a blackboard, a wavy line like a swallow makes skimming a pond for
mosquitoes. In the dream it was late in the evening and we'd been out of
school for years, but there I was in the classroom and its emptiness was
weighing heavy on my heart; it was the 4th of July and we were waiting
for it to get dark outside for the fireworks show, the booms and spirally
sounds we had come to expect. And you were there with me, so I felt
special.

Sometimes I dredge up a feeling I could be feeling but am not just for
the sake of creating a mood. That would be one of my dharma selves,
one of several little color-coded file folders I label 'myself' and keep in a
cabinet in the closet, like a stuffed monkey. Like one of those plastic

half-melting ice-cream bars on specialty shop counters that you reach for even though you know it's a gag. That's me sometimes, feel free to pick me up, call, or stop by and be half-amused, half-annoyed that you are having to listen to my voice when you'd be perfectly content elsewhere, say, in a deer blind smoking cigarettes with the ghost of your father nearby grumbling at you, but you feel the steel of your shotgun against your thigh instead, and that warms your heart. Or, say, just standing by yourself in the middle of a small woods watching the moss grow on the rotting, fallen trees: the sun is going down and it's almost cold enough for you to see your breath, and you imagine it spelling out in the air a long explanation of how people that you had abandoned years ago must have felt, who are now so past forgiving they only think of you when someone brings up your name, an obituary they've seen perhaps of someone with the same last name as yours. You are reading this in your breath in front of you, this explanation that you understand is a projection of your own self-pity, and then you look down and notice that the moss looks greener than you'd ever seen it, and in the branches above some crows begin to caw, reminding you to go home and fix yourself some dinner.

It's those crows I'm talking about, what am I to do about them, they keep appearing in my dreams? Like the one I saw in Chicago: I don't think I've ever been as cold as on that day walking along the lakeshore boardwalk. I didn't know what I was doing there, but I remember looking for you in the waves running up to the shore, trying to be horses with their little white manes. But they were just ponies, merry-go-round ponies, and I was way too old for that. What is it about a purple cloud that pulls me into that death reverie? "What is the universe trying to tell me?"—oh I love to scoff when I hear someone speak that way, but who

25

am I to be the clown stripping off his make-up in front of a whole crowd,
I don't even like to dress up? Here comes that song again in my head
and you aren't here to help me ham it up, you're off doing your smoke
and mirrors trick again, the one we can only speak about in tongues, our
hands in the air as if we're flagging someone down who's just gotten off
an airplane, and it's warm, balmy even, but I can smell the happiness in
the air, it smells like fruit, like watermelon or peaches.

Section 2.

Yearning

I sometimes wonder if as a boy I yearned for things without knowing it, if I had even adopted yearning as the central focus of my being, the light through the fog I'd be driving by the rest of my life, sensing it only as a vague, gray glow that makes everything visible except itself. I wonder if what I was yearning for was a future to match the propensities of my emotion, fill the canyon that I thought formed the depth of my soul. I never suspected the canyon wasn't in my soul, but on some distant planet of my imagination where it rained Mimosa or Japanese Magnolia petals from its crystal-blue skies, and on any one of its nights, warm year-round and smelling of those petals, I would hear a train whistle miles away just before I lapsed into a dream about standing waist-deep in a swimming pool and kissing a large-eyed, full-lipped, ardent lover.

Perhaps the pain of the yearning had driven my every thought, and it was not merely sadness because my ignorance of what I was feeling had turned it into something else, something cruel. It's like trying to call one of your children and the phone turns into a large-mouth bass, the kind your mother would bring home from the Sundays she would go fishing to be alone, to escape the five children she was raising and the office she worked in 8 to 5, to spend a few hours near a small pond, near the katydids screeching, near a distant or not-so-distant mooing of a cow, the burping of a bloated bullfrog or a whole chorus of them singing their absurd arias in the heat, or the far-up-in-the-sky line of exhaust a jet would draw that clarified distance, isolation, and friendlessness. And as you gaze in wonder at this fish in your hand you are reminded of how your mother used to take you with her. She would stand in the scorching heat, cast her line out, then look over to see if yours was taut, your float afloat, and ask you to reel it in to see if you still had bait, and her voice would remind you that you were fishing with her and not standing waist-deep in a swimming pool flirting with the girl of your dreams as she sat lounging poolside in her bathing suit the color of water you'd seen in pictures of the Caribbean.

The girl's hair and eyes would glow with the promise of happiness, but when you see her flirting with your best friend you see in reality that your mother is slipping a worm onto your hook and you ask her when can we go home. Then you realize this too is a dream, that you are home, that your mother hasn't fished in twenty years and may never again. You remember your children, how you watched them swim in pools on hot summer days when they were young, and you look at the palms of your hands and realize that the heat you feel is unbearable, and that the reason your mother sought it out is the reason fishes' rib-bones curve down from their spines and cottonwoods wave their large, open-handed leaves against the sky, clapping their palms together in praise of the very wind that stirs them.

Dream

You dream your mother lies dying on a cot in some makeshift hospital,
a tent perhaps, on the edge of the little town you grew up in, say in
Oklahoma or West Texas. She struggles to get out of her nightgown and
into "something more presentable," she says, and to fix her hair—to put
her unkempt curls back in place like they were when she was a little girl,
she says, growing up in New England, in Vermont, long before she met
your father, before the war, before they wrote letters back and forth when
he was in Italy and fighting his way up the Apennines, long before that.
When she would skate on Lake Champlain and watch the men cut slabs
of ice from it and carry them away in wagons. Your sisters tell her to rest,
that we will take care of her. You go outside into the open air and notice
in the sky two three-headed tornadoes making their way through town—
twin Cerberuses at the gates of hell. They are moving away from you, but
you are concerned for others, for no siren has sounded. You worry for the
town and for your mother, and you marvel at the beauty of the scene, the
muted purples and grays. You marvel that you are witnessing it and that
it is not a dream. Yes, in the dream you marvel that this is not a dream.
You begin to run through the streets with another boy, say a brother
who's now a broker and lives in St. Louis so you don't see him much, but
there he is beside you, a boy like you running in the street alongside these
funnels a few blocks away, these slender, violent ghosts that have wriggled
down like newborns from the bruise-colored clouds.

Memory

In the little Midwestern town I grew up in was a five-and-dime run
by a large German woman who limped. She kept chocolates behind a
glass case, and in the back were shelves full of plastic model airplanes
and ships I only had a few coins for. Memories seem no more than that,
pieces you have to glue together to make into something. There's an
Italian deli in Queens I discovered a couple of years ago—narrow and
stuffed with breads and olive oil, jars of hors d'oeuvres on tall shelves,
salamis and big balls of cheeses hanging on strings from the ceiling. One
person can barely pass another. It was odd to see my father standing in
one of the aisles; he's dead but there he was, reading the label of a jar of
anchovies in his hand—he loved anchovies. He was a foot soldier in Italy
and there were no anchovies in western Oklahoma where he grew up,
and where I, a boy, would lie at night and listen to the train whistle when
the heat, like an insatiable beast after gorging itself all day, had settled
down to sleep. You could feel its exhaustion through the open windows,
its warm breath sucking the curtains against the screen, holding them
there for four, five seconds, then blowing them back out to you, you lying
there watching those curtains move and not knowing they won't move
like that forever. Here I am a boy in this dream, at the edge of a crowd,
squeezing through like a rivulet running to a big river. I can hear it
rushing, can smell the moisture, feel it on my face. I am crying but don't
know why. I can see through the forest of legs a dark hospital room, my
father's feet sticking out from the sheets, tubes on the floor.

Fairgrounds

There you are in your glory, though the battlefield is the county fairgrounds. You hold a ribbon draped over the steer's back. You had ribbons at home, a Purple Heart, distinguished Cross, Silver Star. Your hat shades your face so I can't tell if that's a grin you wear. Where am I looking? Into the steer's ear, it appears, as I hold the halter. I'm not wearing a hat, so the sun blinds me. I must be seven, eight, looking baffled by my own existence, by the sun that fills the blue Oklahoma sky unrelenting, like the animal presence of this seven- or eight-hundred pound beast in my hands. You may be thinking of what calf must be washed and groomed next. I must be thinking of you, or of nothing. Just sensing the smells of the calf, or of you next to me, of the grass, or just listening to the sounds from the barns with their loud blower fans that kept the cattle cool. I remember I liked that shirt I was wearing, the smell of it when it was new, and I liked the way your button-down plaid shirt would stretch across your chest. I could only hope my chest would someday fill out like yours, "barrel-chested" people called you. I was in a barrel, in the barrel of your chest rolling toward a waterfall under an animal sky.

The Nazi Helmet

We never questioned how it came to hang in our garage. We saw them
in movies, symbol of the enemy, its bottom edge down from the ears,
across the base of the neck, shaping an elegance we dared not praise. But
if you got it in the choosing you were lucky and wore it proud, stalking
a friend around corners with a mimosa branch machine gun, a plastic
potato masher poised to blast him off the earth. And even when its walls
banged against your head, your skull like the tongue of a bell, its bottom
edge scraping your ten-year-old shoulders till you felt like you'd drown
in its strange echoes that sent you to the bottom of the Atlantic or the
Mediterranean, or near the Algerian coast where Rommel ruled with
halftracks and desert tanks—even when the summer heat beat on your
head till it boiled like an egg in a pot, even then only a fool surrendered it.
You'd rise from the dead to argue rights: it was *your* daddy with shrapnel
in his back, it hung in *your* garage. But you'd give it up. Like I said, it was
hot, and the weight, like a piano on your head. And you'd want your
friend to experience it. But we never questioned how it came to hang in
our garage. Maybe we feared it was paid for on the voyage home or back
in the states. Not stripped from a sniper as we'd imagined, one who'd
held off your daddy's unit until he, your daddy, could aim his M-1 and
drop that sniper from the tree like a plump dove.

New Cocktails

In a dream last night my father was alive and I was in Chios City sipping cocktails with friends on a veranda, staring across the Aegean at the coast of Turkey. It all seemed very real. Everyone was speaking Greek and testing a drink made with scotch called Little Death, which calls for tea made from damiana leaves and a teaspoon of raspberry jam: add the scotch, shake in ice, serve over ice, sprinkling the damiana leaves on top. We were all gazing at the water when we heard the ferry horn blast, our heads turning as one to catch a glimpse of the tourists cascading down the ramp and into the city, where, as in Venice, the bay water comes right up to the streets and laps at them like cats' tongues. Someone nearby quoted the last lines of *The Great Gatsby*, something about sailing inevitably into the past, and I said to no one in particular that those lines remind me of a gin cocktail called Fountain of Youth: a dash of Pimm's, white cranberry juice, a bit of lime, thin slices of muddled cucumber. Everyone said ooh and ahh as if it were a joke we only had to think of to make us laugh. Then I noticed an old girlfriend, was it Sherry, Debbie, Stephanie? A confluence of all three? She was all in black, a silk crepe-de-chine dress with a black veil over her face and decolette. Behind her were two soldiers, medals pinned to their chests, and as they pointed their rifles at the sky I saw a fresh grave between them and understood this to be my father's funeral, my father who landed at Anzio in '44 and fought the Germans up the Apennines. How could this be, I thought? Then the old girlfriend leaned over and whispered in my ear, "Relax, the Buddha has arthritic hands," and the scent of her perfume and of the cocktail on her breath made me want to kiss her. She walked to the mound, hiked up her dress, and straddled it. The soldiers fired their rifles into the air and it was loud and shocking. I took another sip of Fountain of Youth, or was it Little Death, and watched her spiked heels sink into the dirt beside the grave. I looked up and saw a faraway jet crawling across the sky like a wounded insect. I caught her eye and nodded, as if to say I knew what she meant about the Buddha.

Bus Trip

.

It's mid-afternoon in mid-winter, a five-hour trip across upstate New York, and there's snow on the ground and draping the hillside trees. The sun's going down already behind some purple clouds that look like they could be over northern Pennsylvania or the Land of Oz take your pick. The driver seems to take this beautiful scenery in stride as if he were walking home through some woods, not rushing really but with deliberation nonetheless, rubbing his bald head, looking left, right, fidgeting his big body and working the oversized steering wheel. There's a young woman across the aisle from me with a star on her right hand the size of a silver dollar, maybe a tattoo maybe a bar last night I don't know. She's sprawled out on the seat now, exposing her lower back, nothing sexy just lower back skin. It's in the 30s or 40s outside and lots of heads in here are leaning against the windows—I assume they're finding the slight chill of the glass refreshing given the stuffiness in here. The bus's engine is humming and somewhere in the back someone's cell phone rings, softly, like in a dream. There's something primal going on here the way we're all relaxing and without thinking about it trusting this one man to look over us, to keep us safe from the vagaries of fate, the whims of harm and the errant thoughts of our inevitable demise. Lord knows I can talk with the best of them when I get warmed up, but it occurs to me that in the context of the inherent vulnerability of this mortal coil it is important not to say more than is called for, ever.

Snowflakes

Stonewall Jackson was never scared, we're told, but he did ride his horse sometimes with one arm up because he thought it kept him straight in the saddle. I think I'll take that up, walk around with one arm in the air—tell people it keeps me on my horse. They might ask, "Where's your horse?" which is the question I will have been waiting for. I will say my horse is the earth and if you don't walk with one arm up you may fall into the abyss, which we have a word for but which by definition has no meaning. So much of language, I'll continue, has no meaning and yet we talk on and on, our words like snowflakes piling onto themselves, long after we've watched them out our windows like contented cats. I'll say the snowflakes keep falling, quietly of course, but like a timer going off for something we'd forgotten. And because they're quiet we can't hear them, but they keep falling long after we've fallen asleep.

At the Old Castle Hotel

How fortunate we were to hear the geese before sunup. Like a waterfall
their honking dropped into the lake outside our window and rose to our
room in a fine mist. We told ourselves it was the mist of history. The
breakfast downstairs was well attended. On the mantel above the blue-
and-white porcelain bowls of maple syrup were puppets dressed as court
jesters and below them a knight in a suit of armor the color of dark
coffee. This is a castle after all, we thought to ourselves, history echoing
off its walls: hissing torches in the halls, Provencal peasants singing
outside in the sun, screams from the Inquisition rising from the cellar.
We took a walk and removed our gloves in the strong wind to touch
the bark of the trees, the big willows near the lake's shore. They hang
their heads and brace against the wind like geese in flight. All history's
backdrop is nature, they remind us, a source of succor and the object of
all our prayers. I had dreamed the night before of playing poker with a
favorite uncle who likes to smoke cigars, tell jokes, and pray. He's old now,
sore hips and knees and can't eat bacon like he used to. He too is history,
bracing against the cold, walking through the air as if in a suit of armor.
I woke to the smell of bacon and thought maybe the knight will knock
on our door to deliver breakfast, pick up the check even, and thank us
for keeping up appearances. In return we'll tell him how the windstorm
outside made us feel ostracized to the moon. Or how we came back to
find our room flooded with the heat of a fake fireplace, how the clean
towels sat perched on the bed like white chickens roosting, or cheetahs in
trees on a hot Pleistocene night. It'll be our contribution, I thought, the
story of how the large cats' satiate bellies bulged on the branches, their
tails like snakes weaving up through the night. We'll say they had stuffed
themselves with the flesh of history.

On Moral Egalitarianism

Driving home from work I think about the child's song "the wheels on
the bus go round and round." I think how wheels spin faster than we can
imagine, and silent as planets! That's not in the song, I think to myself.
I sit in my car, watching somnolently as the weather goes by, a gray
afternoon between two Finger Lakes. A few miles away on both sides of
me, the landscape near the lakes slopes down to water and makes the
weather there good for grapes—winters less cold, summers less hot, the
grapes good for wine, wine good for weddings and toasts and elegant
meals. People on the world go round and round, and children sing about
it and about themselves, and to me they're singing about winter and
the way its light changes into spring like a child's voice growing out of
itself. And winter's end is near, the last flakes of the season swirling like
conclusions near my living room window, bumping against the glass as
if trying to break in, to offer themselves as the last paragraph, the last
sentence, before the book closes. Right outside the window, the branches
of the decades-old maple tree are sketched clearly against the sky's
gray, like an artist's strokes on a gray canvass, like rivers on a map. The
branches do not judge, nor do they sketch themselves, as I am doing here.
I am fifty-six and cannot separate myself from my deeds. I am what I
have done, and what I do every day. The wind is howling now whistling
through the house like a ghost, like the way I'd whistle walking past a
graveyard imagining my mother six feet under there and playing bridge
with her neighborhood friends, all of them propped up on their elbows
and complaining about their arthritis and the piss-poor cards in their
boney hands. I imagine suddenly being ghostly myself and drifting vault
to vault serving manhattans, gin and tonics, whatever they want to allay
their deep and unabated thirst.

Late April and It's Snowing

One night in the fall of '88, over three feet of snow fell in the mid-Hudson Valley on the full-leaved branches in their beauty, the golds and crimsons and all the blends of colors that astounded my wife and me on our daily walks in those early years of our love. We woke the next morning to shotgun-blasts of branches snapping outside our window, walked out to see they had barely missed our house and car, framing them and transforming the yard into a kind of natural disaster folk art. We had typically wakened to squirrels playing field hockey in the attic or to crows outside speaking their minds in mid-flight. That morning, and for several days afterwards without power in the house, we assumed a kind of primitive life, an ironic privilege, we thought. Our daughter was born the following year. We have long since divorced, my daughter's mother and I, our correspondence limited now to money talk and small recriminations that leave me thinking how short life is. I think of a conductor's baton raised, someone coughing in a quiet concert hall. What happens to that moment of anticipation that compels us to begin it all, to have children, raise them?

Lately I think of courtship as the prime ruse of the species. Where does that leave my own self-regard, having been, of course, a child myself, presumably the pulsing consequence of one of my mother and father's amorous moments. My mother tells the story of sitting down and crying upon hearing of her pregnancy with me, her fifth. Not tears of joy, I say to myself when I hear this, as though upon her retelling I must confirm for myself what her tears meant. My mother's sorrow was simply a sub-plot of the story of life, what drives production, an economist might say. My father liked to teach me to crack boiled eggs just right, in the middle with a knife, scooping them out just so. I see him at the stove, two eggs boiling in a pot, and when I find myself in the same spot in my own kitchen, he a dozen years dead now, I think of the eggs as before and after, and when cracked and scooped into a bowl, cause and effect. Then I sprinkle cause and effect with salt and pepper and down them with toast and jam.

I miss my children. It's difficult to get them to return my calls. I think of a dog I had as a child, and in my mind I watch her resting her head on my lap. I missed that blind intimacy until a few years back I got another just like her for my wife. Yesterday on the bus-ride home from work, I watched the back of a woman's head with her hair neatly twirled in a bun. I thought to myself, nothing is not spun by grief.

"Ellipse"

A breeze eases into my living room this morning, a pleasant mid-June breeze, my window up, screens installed. Japanese Magnolia blooms dropped weeks ago just in time to usher in flowering wisteria, and the leaves on the bushes and trees next to the house, that later in the year will be blown from their branches, are young green faces now, just coming into the world, alongside fleshy-globed peonies and azaleas in the neighborhood gardens, the last of the lilacs and the short-lived poppies, morning glories, and along the suburban paths birdsfoot trefoil, buttercups, purple phlox—words, so many words for things, ideas. They're like dry leaves themselves, in my mind, these words, tearing from my memory at the slightest breeze. Ellipse is one, somehow more elusive than most for me. Perhaps it evokes loss, of those no longer with me: grandparents, parents, a nephew three-days old, my wife's mother at forty-seven. I'd like to see it drift toward the sun like a balloon I've let go of, growing smaller and smaller.

The Last Out

I heard later the Yankees blew it in the bottom of the ninth. In the top of the inning one of the Royals had hit a homer off Rivera to make it 3-2 and then with bases loaded Cabrera bounced out to first. I'd seen most of the game, saw A-Rod's homer in the bottom of the eighth that tied it up, but my wife and I had to get to the park before it got too dark, to grill all the vegetables and cool ourselves in the breezes off the water, and to enjoy the last of the purple clouds. While we watched the sunset I reminisced about this park twenty-five years ago, how I'd written a poem about it in which I used the word *promontory* even though the park has no promontory to speak of, because I thought the sound of the word evoked the image of the willows hanging their green growth down against the sky's dying light. I told her I used to think words could do that, reify nature's beauty, but that I'm glad words in my mind have been unburdened of that gravitas. She was turning the vegetables—egg plants whole and cut up, zucchini and onions, red and green peppers—and I was watching the dog. I talked about my former vision of success, how if you paid attention to the details good things will happen. "Yeah," she said, "I used to think that too," a response that pleased me. And yet for a moment I had a yearning that the vision be true again, and that her existence in my life be its proof, that my devotion and our love were the details well attended to. When they replayed the game the next day there I was again, A-Rod had hit the homer, tied again, Rivera came out and gave up that home run; bottom of the ninth, A-Rod on base, Giambi walks, bases loaded with two outs and Cabrera up with the tying run on third. Then came a storm alert and by the time the TV came back on the players were walking off the field.

But for the Grace

Early September, late afternoon, and on the north side of the house
sunlight has squeezed between heavy foliage and spilled itself in small
puddles on the lawn. From my second floor window I watch a man
on a ladder scrape the side of his house preparing it for paint, each
movement precarious, each step. I think to myself a metaphor's vehicle
sometimes over-runs its mark. The puddles, for example, are not spilled
paint signaling the painter's fall, but a projection of my own dread and
self-congratulation. We spin our webs wide to catch our fears and our
good regard. If only a vehicle were mere vehicle, that even just today I
could keep myself from behind the wheel like we do drunks. If only the
scruffy-bearded old man I saw yesterday crouched under a bridge on
the outskirts of town as I drove by were his own man, no tool for my
psychological machinations—and that were he to hitch a ride into town
to beg on main street I could make his cup clink with that generous
thought.

The Girl from Ipanema

I have headphones on listening to it on repeat, sitting in my living room with the windows open, Getz's sax lazy and relaxed, cool as a martini. Sunlight slips between the leaves, a new light, late summer, different from early and mid-summer light. It's afternoon and the birds have been quiet all day, even the crows. These days birds are most of the neighborhood's traffic and most car traffic is slow and easy. Even so, sometimes when we walk I feel as if I'm Jonah and cars are about to swallow me. On our walk this morning—my wife and I—our only concern was whether to go straight on the sunny street and visit the white llama down the road, endure some traffic, or turn right and come back down quieter Cayuga street.

We went straight and came back straight, the traffic was light, and the llama didn't rise, kept chewing in the middle of the field. Some days we catch her walking in the field like the girl from Ipanema, oblivious to our admiration of her beauty here in upstate New York, lost in a lovely cloud of unknowing. Some days she walks to the fence to rest her head on the top rail and follow us, as if we were all tethered.

On the way back from our walk we gathered some Black-eyed Susans from the roadside wildflowers—purple vetch, Cornflowers, Queen Anne's lace. When we got back I finished digging out a root at the edge of the drive, big around as my arm, making room to replace a landscaping log. The root was part of a tree that fell on the house last year. Funny how the root of a dead tree, like an old grievance or love, can still make its presence known, heaving everything above it on its back with its slow strength—grass, gravel, landscaping logs. I had worked three days to loosen the dirt around it and today it gave way to my saw. I joked with a neighbor that it was my white whale, but I wasn't thinking how much it actually looked like one, rising up to the surface to sun its back. It's still cool this afternoon, in the low 70s, and it rained last night so it's cool from the rain as well, cool as the girl from Ipanema, cool as a gin and tonic and going down almost as easy.

The Life of Spaces

A friend's poems have me thinking about places as beings. He and I
bicycled around the DelMarva peninsula years ago and while camping at
Rehobeth Beach we learned of German prisoners of war buried nearby.
It gave the space a life we hadn't expected. My older siblings tell me of
a creek we used to play in outside our neighborhood when I was almost
too young to remember—it was the Washita River—and I don't know if
I remember it, that space on the Washita, like I don't know if I remember
some old relatives I've heard stories about. Old relatives would sometimes
respond to me so familiarly it was as if their remembering was working
for both of us. My paternal grandfather Michael Brown's brother, for
example, great uncle Clarence, came up to me at a family reunion when
I was a kid—I was standing shell-shocked in a crowd of relatives—smiled
and shook my hand and said my name like he'd known me his whole
life, and now when I see his grave near my mother's and father's I feel
his handshake and hear his voice, see his smile. I feel the space around
his gravestone remembering me, taking on a liveliness I want to speak
to. Some cultural anthropologists say the religious ethos of our ancient
ancestors was mostly punitive, that the punishments and occasional
rewards came, according to these cultures, not in an afterlife but in the
here and now of earthly life, meted out from those already in the afterlife,
dead ancestors and other spirits. Behave badly and these spirits would
destroy your crops, make fish not bite, kill your beloved dog or, worse,
your child. They say our religious ethos is more a reward system, that
God is now less a punisher than a model of loving kindness, and now
we're morally enlightened because our ethical sphere includes not just
fellow tribesmen but all people. But what about spaces? Do we behave as
nicely to spaces as our ancestors did, who moved only as fast as their feet
would take them? When I'm walking along a road, with my dog usually,

enjoying the purple knapweed and fall cosmos and asters, or it's winter and I'm trying not to slip on ice, I'm offended when cars don't slow down in recognition of me there on foot, unprotected by steel or speed. They'll zoom past at 40, 50, 60 miles an hour. Maybe all spaces feel toward cars as I do then, offended that they move so fast through them. Slow down, they would say if they could, you're hurting my feelings.

Autumn Lament

I lie in bed this morning with two poems in my lap: one a black and
white-striped clarity authored by sunlight slicing through the blinds, its
central image a zebra calf resting from a long night of hiding from lions,
or from very ambitious chimpanzees. Or maybe it's a human ribcage
laid bare and sprawled across me like a lover, part of a skeleton the rest
of which is ghostly and barely visible, the skull on the pillow next to me,
the boney feet dangling off to the side, we two basking in a hot afternoon
post-coital high. The other is Richard Wilbur prattling about lilacs: "But
the sun suddenly/settled about them,/And green and grateful/they grew,
Healed in that hush/that hospital quiet." The first is conspicuous in its
silence and odorlessness, the second's in love with its own alliteration,
a perfumed poetics. I myself am weary of writing poems, a chicken
pecking in the dust, for words will never bring back my mother dead
last month, nor did they for her hers when she was five. What wafting
scent words fail to conjure anyway is worth the effort when it's death's
smell we're left with ever after? I don't mean the stink, though that reality
was true for eons before embalming, such that now we don't even get
that rank pleasure, the shock of knowing you're alive when something
you loved is not, the last gift of the dead. No, I'm referring to a shock
analogous to that though opposing in its truth: that since we are not in
the end with anyone we are nothing, wordless poems, blank and odorless
images. But such a testament flies in my face, for this is a poem, and for
my mother no less, who would've scoffed at such narcissistic nihilism. She
herself dealt with loss stoically, going about her days with an industrious
generosity that opened out from her as a force unstrained, like a blue
tulip, or a lilac.

Celebrating Your Life

After a violent week in the Gaza strip it's calm there again, the cease-fire in effect. Let's celebrate the cease-fire. But it's December and gray outside, and I can sense you're picturing a nuclear winter. I sense you're picturing a nuclear winter because I can count on your worry that without that dark side I might be trying to slip one by you, make you think the world's rosier than it is, that God is smiling down on us in our silly stew of nuclear winter apprehension. We should let Him smile down on us, you're afraid I'll tell you, because without Him we are nothing, peas in a pod rotting on a vine. But perhaps you're afraid of being told you're a pea in a pod rotting on the vine without Him, that it's okay to be rotting on the vine without Him. Your happiness will be that of two peas in a pod, happy to be like each other and in a pod together, even if rotting, for in their similarity they are not alone. But I'm not two people, you'll retort, and you're afraid I'll respond, but you are, and as such not alone. You are you and that other you you are always talking to, debating with, arguing whether or not to eat that ice cream, to do that or not do that, to give up the change or not in your pocket at the sound of that little bell ringing outside the liquor store you're about to drop fifty bucks in. You two bicker like an old married couple, your hair getting thin and gray together. You two bicker so much if people could see you as the two people you actually are, eating from the same spoon, making each other coffee in the morning, if only they could see you at home they'd say you're two peas in a pod. You're afraid I'll tell you to celebrate that. You're two peas in a pod rotting on the vine together and it's a glorious pod you're rotting in. That's what you're afraid I'll say. And you're afraid I'll say plenty of fine organic matter has rotted on the vine in our lifetimes, not to mention in the long stretch of earthly life. I'm thinking of apples in the grass just down the road from here migrant workers neglected. I'm thinking of apples that hang over streets and drop and get run over, apple road-kill. I'm picturing wild blueberries in Maine nobody ever sees. I'm picturing lobsters and crabs that die at the bottom of the ocean and disintegrate. I'm picturing the Permia-Triassic extinction 250 million years ago that killed off 96% of all marine species and 70% of all terrestrial vertebrate species. You're afraid I'll extol the virtues of going extinct, that I'll implore you to celebrate it, rejoice in it, because extinction has been the fate of almost every living species that has ever lived, and when you're a member of that club you won't be alone, that is, if you can consider yourself a you still. And if not, isn't that something to celebrate as well, you're afraid I'll say. You—or what used to be you—will join the club of nothingness, the nothingness that lives forever, so to speak. You're afraid of that "so to speak," afraid it means the celebration I'm asking of you isn't real. You're afraid what I'm asking you to celebrate is your own demise. To get up on your hind legs like an ant before he gets stepped on. A little ant sees he's getting stepped on and rises up on his hind legs to do a little ant dance. You're afraid I'm going to say that ant is you. And that that little dance, if only you could see it as such, is your life.

Section 3.

Something He Read

There are willows in the park down the street whose leaves, when the wind blows, appear to flow down like tears. The green curtains are drawn. I walk to the dresser and lift the photograph to my cheek. There is no child in the house. I dream of storms and rescues, and still there is no child. Trucks growl outside; I hear the wind pick up and picture the backyard poppies being blown about, their scarlet heads tossed as if on ocean waves, the kind just off shore that when you're swimming among them lift you up for a second or two and then drop you. Love is a dying word, I think to myself, and then remember something I read, something about the gravity of memory. The forecast is rain, dark clouds in the sky. I look in the mirror at the creases on my face, like folds on paper airplanes—down down the gravity of memory.

Ghosts

To ask what a counter-rationalist poetry would look or sound like
may be like asking what it's like to live underwater, or to bathe while
floating in outer space, or to be dead. Amusing to imagine, but difficult
to experience, precisely because it's beyond our experience, and as
empiricism tells us experience is our only teacher. I suppose we might see
ourselves as ghosts haunting the technocratic world: in it but not of it.
Making our little haunting sounds, but only vaguely heard by the living,
if heard at all—certainly not seen, sometimes wondered about perhaps,
like children wondering about the center of the earth or what's beyond
the sky or later in their lives the known universe. And sometimes sitting
alone and listening to the sunlight fall like rain on a perfect afternoon
in April, I wonder if what it is I perceive as poison is what has always
been poison, which means it has always been sunlight or rain pure as
a golden little giggle from a three-year-old child who hasn't known yet
what empiricism is or what might grow in her brain someday to be
sadness and distance and pain, or to be the fear of being left by the one
thing she doesn't know yet is all she ever wanted, that is, someone to sing
lalalalalala in her ear, quietly and without shame or remorse, with one
hand stroking her hair and the other the inside of her arm. Just don't
speak, she says, then stands up from her crib, grows up, and floats around
like the rest of us, bent over from the weight of her dead bones and from
the sounds that had accumulated in her head for years. Just don't speak,
she tries to say again years later, but the words only come out in muted
colors like in clouds over a stormy ocean, so far off to the south that it
makes her want to be there and not here on a white sandy beach, where
she stands with her father or her lover, or both. Or maybe the words
come out in the smells of a breakfast cooking over an outdoor fire, bacon
perhaps, perhaps just eggs with toast a little burnt on one side, but

with butter and peach jam she won't taste the poison. Or maybe the words come out in the way gravel felt on her bare feet in the summer as she was trying to cross the road to get to the pond her mother told her to stay away from because she wasn't a good swimmer. It's all in the way you ask the question, her mother used to tell her, and in the tone of your voice just before you pass away into candyland. That's when it will dawn on her that though losing everything isn't all it's been cracked up to be, it's all we ever had.

Memento Mori

Sometimes when I read or hear a poem, I'll drift up and out—there I go floating on a raft down some mild whitewater, trees and sky lifting me out of my petty anxieties, beer stashed safely in the cooler. So when the cool purple-blue of a stove's pilot light appeared in a poem I was listening to online, two sisters doing dishes in its glow and whispering about a preemie born out of wedlock, I was there, or here I should say, in my head, burnt match in hand, my father teaching me to boil an egg. And in my imagination I watched the match-head's smoke lift up like a snake to the poem's flute music. Then that Holstein appeared, the one that lay for three days with her uterus turned inside out out back of the barn, a smoky purple-blue in the sky behind her, nothing to do but stitch her up and hope she recovers but she doesn't. Then comes her dead calf beside her, earlier, and then, finally, the yellow tractor to dig a hole and shovel them both into it. That happens sometimes too, the opposite of rising up and out.

Boy Survives Half Hour Underwater

How do you wrap a warm blanket around the unknowable and put it to bed? And when it becomes a headline in both *The New York Times* and *The Post* can you walk away a witness to it and begin thinking of other things? Such as the I Do at a wedding in which the preacher asks science do you take religion and believe her no questions asked, no microscopic details to verify her fidelity? And you, religion, do you promise to believe in the sanctity of disbelief, to eat what's in the Petri dish he will set in front of you every night till death do you part? Then you can divorce, split the assets, and promise to love the boy you've abandoned who occasionally asks the other orphans to ask him again what it was like to die and live again, and they will all roll their eyes and say shut up we've got our own problems. And all he can hear is The Then, the dark cold voices in his head and the pounding in his chest telling him to remember what had just happened, as if it were a movie he'd just seen that had a plot and clear voices with a celebrity or two who spoke in a language he understood, with blood and dilation and capillary pressure and all the numb ugliness of pain, the oxygen incessantly pumping in his head where even the unthinkable emerges like Lazarus. But it'll never happen again, he knows it, up from the cold water where it was toasty and delicious, where there was not a single syllable to hail the coming of the angels.

Spring Training

We're told some structures in the brain did not exist before the alphabet, created by the writing system the Greeks believed they'd borrowed from the Phoenicians. These new structures impelled the brain to go beyond itself, to arrive at more complex thought processes, consciousness of self and others and consciousness of consciousness itself. Socrates was suspicious of writing because it doesn't yield the extemporaneous give and take of speech he thought essential to nurturing true knowledge, its tonalities, inflections, shades of meaning that swerve in large or small arcs like a swallow up and over small ponds in summer, diving for mosquitoes or other insects. Socrates thought himself a kind of mosquito on the horse-ass of Athenian citizenry, and they killed him, of course, they said because he didn't believe in god and had corrupted the youth. He believed in god, though; he just believed you got close to him by being in touch with your own better nature, i.e., your reasoning nature, questioning every assumption until you got to the essence of the thing—truth, justice, beauty. Outside my office window beautiful young men are playing baseball, and beyond them cars and trucks hurrying by on the ugly highway. It is gray and late winter, early spring. Spring is on the tip of everyone's tongue, and on the tips of limbs and bushes as if they had tongues themselves ready to burst out their stiff meanings, spew out apologetics and disquisitions full of freely-labeled concepts such as pain, pleasure, and virtue. Forsythia, for example, sit up anxious to sprout their yellow hope and spout a future I didn't ask for. And all the new green leaves morning noon and night are whispering "life!" "growth!," insinuating into our lives their colorful categories, imposing on the world their facile *prima facie*. I hate abstractions, hate them all.

If Time is a Phantom

What is it with poems that use the phrase 'right now'? Such as "I
think I feel good about myself right now." They surely can't refer
to the moment of our reading, so we're presumably being asked to
appreciate the immediacy of the writer's emotion when he or she wrote
it, weeks, months, even years before our reading it. Doesn't that elapsed
time undermine what we're being asked to appreciate? How can you
champion immediacy when long lapses of time pass between the writing
and reading? Is it worth it—this attempt at authenticity—is it worth it
to ignore those realities just to place us inside the poet's head? What's
so great about immediacy anyway? Why do we think it's the holy grail
of experience? Isn't it in truth a phantom? When does it happen? Now?
Now's gone already; in fact, it never was: even as I was typing it, it was
never there. Not when I typed the n, or the o, or the w, and it surely
wasn't there when I'd typed all three. Even the phrase "gone already"
is misleading since it implies that the moment I was trying to capture
had eluded me at some point between typing and not typing. But that
moment had never existed! So what we think is the fundamental element
of experience is an illusion: there is no now, and therefore no before or
after. What then are we to do with our experiences of, say, love? How can
we say I love you and mean it when the moments in which it's felt and
expressed never existed? Perhaps it's time to embrace unknowing and
accept the consequent vulnerability. Time to look at the purple Million
Bells for long stretches; run our hands through the rosemary as if stroking
a cat and walk down the street together smelling the scent it leaves in our
palms; time to watch the night sky together and when the clouds clear
try to point out Orion or Cassiopeia and when we fail fathom ourselves
children again and point to the big dipper imagining it full of ice cream,
the other stars sprinkles or white chocolate chips; time to walk to the

train track on a summer evening, take off our shoes and feel the warmth of the track on the soles of our feet; to walk out into the yard a moment before retiring to bed, bend down to feel the grass, then stand and remark to ourselves how ironic it is there's no such thing as time and yet our backs are not what they used to be. Time to disavow our grief for time's passing.

Intelligence

You might think I think highly of myself with such a title, that I'm about
to address what I have prior knowledge of or own. A person knows how
to play a sport well and we say he or she's got game. Well, I'm here to
say that for intelligence I've begun to suspect I ain't got jack, destitute
as a hole in the ground, dumb as a muffin. Dumb as a fence post, as the
phrase goes, though when I think about it longer than a wink I picture
that post doing a pretty smart job holding up not just a fence but the very
idea of one. The something there is that doesn't love a wall may be more
than groundswell, as Mr. Frost tells us, but where would all that boundary
theory be without the wall itself? I'm nowhere near smart as a post.
What caused this crisis? you might ask. Who knows? One day you think
you know a thing or two, own this or that, can rattle off rules about, say,
modifiers and comma splices, the next day it's modifiers that own you:
quick, slow, handsome, plain as asphalt, accomplished, loser—say what
you will, that's me, no more determinant of my own status than a piece
of clay in a child's hand. And comma splices? My own behind's spliced
and still all of a piece—why can't a comma cleave a couple of cheeky
clauses? I'm afraid I've lost the sense of what intelligence is. Some think it
quickness of thought. I'm slow as molasses in Alaska, get tongue-tied just
saying hello on the telephone and can't think on my feet quick enough
to say goodbye back before whoever on the other end hangs up. Some
think it's deep thought. I'm shallow as a sidewalk puddle, wouldn't know
deep standing in the Grand Canyon. My dog stares at me when she has
to pee—you communicate with another species and you can call yourself
Albert Abraham Lincoln Einstein. But I'll forget—she'll stare and stare
and I'll think all she wants is the leftover milk in my cereal bowl, and the
other day after a good hour of it she crawled up on my lap and peed on
me—dumb as a bedpan I am. Maybe it's something else altogether,

like wisdom, which, like happiness, can't be got till you're dead, as old Solon warned us. That is, fortune quick as a wink can turn wisdom into dumb as a doornail. I say call no one wise till they're dressed to the nines in beetles and worms.

Ode to Shame

I'm standing in front of a cash register at a coffee shop near my office,
holding in my left hand the penny cup and in my right a few quarters
I just retrieved from my pocket. I'm gripping the quarters with the last
three digits of my hand because with my thumb and forefinger I'm
trying to fish some pennies out of the cup, two to be exact, for a $1.07
purchase of a cup of vanilla pudding topped with whipped cream and
a maraschino cherry. As I go for the two pennies with my thumb and
forefinger I see a nickel in the cup, so I think what the hell I'll take
the whole seven cents because I'd prefer to carry in my pocket as little
change as possible and because few transactions in life resolve themselves
as cleanly as this one is about to, and that it's resolving itself with free
money will make the exchange quintessentially satisfying, and I think to
myself that this experience could even manifest as a small pleasure. So
with thumb and forefinger I'm gathering the three coins—the nickel and
two pennies—when the cashier says, "the change cup is for when you
need a penny or two, not for the whole purchase." You see, I'm a regular,
and this cashier has admonished me before, for saying "small coffee"
upon placing my travel cup on the counter when in her judgment its size
warrants my paying for medium. I told her once, charging the ramparts,
that I intend to fill my cup up only so high, that even then I rarely drink
it all and that the one or two inches in the bottom often go forgotten and
since I typically add cream, well, the little leftover puddle often grows
mold and I'd rather not have moldy coffee on my desk for days on end.
But she wouldn't have any of it, and I retreated that day vowing in the
future to say "small" only when someone else was defending the register.
So as she's admonishing me for digging into the cup longer than it takes
to extract from it one or two coins as opposed to three, I begin thinking
about the morality of taking out of the cup seven cents versus two, and

I'm thinking it doesn't really matter because it's only a nickel and, besides, it's there in the penny cup, which name, by the way, I begin to think to myself, fails to signify the cup's full function given there's often silver in it. But hey, I continue thinking to myself, words often signify something different than what they're typically intended to, such as, say, when a bus that's filling in for a broken-down 8:15 train is referred to as the 8:15 train, or when a homeless man's piece of cardboard he sleeps under is referred to as his house. I'm thinking how this fluidity of signification can create moral problems. Orwell had something to say about this, calling for an imperative to match the names of things or actions with their moral import or intent. We allow seemingly innocuous ambiguous linguistic signifiers and before we know it we're calling innocent civilians killed in military strikes "collateral damage" or "insurgents." I'm thinking all this when I inadvertently drop into the cup one of the quarters from my hand, a natural occurrence given that I'm attempting to secure three coins with two digits of a hand that's gripping several quarters, and without thinking about it—because I'm distracted by the admonishment and the morality of 5 vs. 2 and the moral issues accruing from the fluidity of linguistic signification—I reach into the cup and retrieve what I'm assuming is rightfully mine, the quarter. Unfortunately the cashier witnesses this heinous act of piracy, and in front of several witnesses loudly calls me out on it. I immediately and just as loudly defend myself: "I dropped the quarter in there!" Which defense of course makes me appear as guilty as Jesse James holding a smoking gun in one hand, a wad of cash in the other, a train full of screaming women and children behind me, dead men dangling out the coach windows. As I walk away I scold her for assuming my guilt. "How could you!" I say, infusing my incredulity with self-righteousness. But seconds later, my heart palpitating,

I'm asking myself, did I really drop the quarter or was it already in there? I don't remember seeing it in the cup before I think I dropped it, but I could've missed it because I was focused on the nickel. Should I admit, I ask myself, that when I snatched it up I was possibly looking for a quick little income boost, intuiting that since no one would notice it was eminently permissible? Or should I just resolve to assume it was mine, if for no other reason than to liberate myself from the defensiveness created by my own self-suspicion?

The Death of Keats

I watched that new movie about him last night, cried my eyes out and went straight to a Mexican bar with friends and ordered a taco and a double scotch. Then I went home, poured myself a White Russian and watched a football game, then went to bed and dreamed I suffered an emotional breakdown, checked myself in and that was it, said goodbye to friends and resigned myself to months of pill popping and group therapy. When I woke, it was autumn, the season of mists and mellow fruitfulness, and aside from the slight hangover I felt great. I thought to myself, I have to remember to drink more water before I go to bed on nights like that. I looked outside and it was misty, which simply meant I wouldn't be taking any leisurely jogs through the park with my dog because she hates this kind of weather. I decided today would be the day I'd take a cigar out on the back porch and watch for nightingales in the dusk.

Dare

Let's sprawl our bodies across a busy highway and see who screams uncle first. Let's hold our feet in icy water for a whole as-long-as-it-takes-to-get-painful and call it pleasure. Let's think what thoughts we're supposed to think, then bury them in feces in our mind's eye. Let's listen to what sounds like ice skates slicing their way up a freshly frozen river, and to what we imagine we'd be hearing if we held our ears to that ice, how we might not hear anything but the occasional crack that foretells our demise. Let's listen to the music of those cracks, how they scream like a mother protecting her young. Let's take meaning itself, drink it like it's tequila and we're standing at the edge of a cliff in Brazil waiting for the tide to come in so we can take the swan dive that reveals we've evolved from single-celled organisms. Let's imagine the gray clouds rolling above the lake I'm watching right now are buffalo, or floating manatees, or large-mouth bass cruising for a meal. Let's cruise for a meal in a homeless shelter and ask around for theories of poetry. Let's hold our breaths and listen as if we were living under a bridge in Albuquerque or Detroit and what we were about to hear would feed us, a whole meal perhaps, lamb stew with home made bread. Let's listen with bellies full as if we'd forsaken ourselves, as if the world understood us on its own terms.

Nice Day

Seventy-six degrees in August, all the limbs on the massive maples in the back yard are smiling, albeit crookedly. The smiles are what we call wry smiles and these limbs are nothing if not wry. They reach up and out like a long-snouted dog sticking its nose in the air to catch a scent. I think they smell maybe a dead rat or the compost barrel in the yard or the deer shit pile near it. The sky, mid-afternoon partly cloudy, looks on from above and smells everything and nothing, preoccupied with its own impatience, for fall, that is. You can see it in its face, the anticipated excitement of all those blustery days ahead. We've lost our only key to the car, but several cases of home-made strawberry jam are in the basement. I'm so happy today I could cut off my head and stick it in the garden to grow.

The God of Absence

I look at the trees outside my window today, mid-fall, their leaves turning yellow and turning literally lighter, often dry and crisp almost before they're blown off the branch, their edges curling up and forming little tubes of air for flight. Branches lighter too from less moisture, and I imagine the limbs of those trees with the passing of summer, in response to this gradual shift in weight they must bear, having slowly turned hollow as well, as if transforming into toy models of themselves. I'm remembering plastic model airplanes from my childhood, how light and full of air they were. Perhaps modern flight is an homage to absence, large fuselages of loneliness and intimations of mortality. But it could also be a form of meditation. To walk into those whales is to swim into the bowels of all myth, to breathe in for a few hours the invigorating air of emptiness.

Omnitude

I've prepared some beds in the back yard for garlic but haven't planted yet because we haven't had a frost, though the leaves are getting yellower and yellower on the 100-year-old silver maples back there. I hear these maples are called widow-makers because the limbs get drier than most and are susceptible to breaking off if an early snow catches them with leaves still on. We were directly under them, standing by the garlic beds, when my wife told me this the other day as she was also telling me of an expected snowstorm. I looked up like Scarecrow does when Dorothy first mentions the witch, but my next thought was that I'm glad they aren't called widower-makers, because I'd rather it be me—I'd rather she not die at all. Funny thing about accidental death, though, I think of it as something I'd see coming, but I wouldn't. In the split second it's happening maybe I'd think this is an accident and I could be hurt, but I wouldn't imagine I wouldn't live through it. Life subsumes all thought.

Ars Poetica

I would like to leave the page blank, but I'm afraid it would all be
misunderstood or, worse, forgotten. It's late and the clock is ticking,
the dog snores, and the pencil, well, it seems to have a mind of its own,
like a music box wound up. I had one once, a gift from my mother—
the key turned and turned and notes fell into my ears or rose to them
if the box was in my hand, say, waist-level in my hand, where it sat
inanimate and yet alive with feeling and warmth, its smooth wooden lid
not yet stained with age. I didn't recognize its tune then, an incantation
from a time before my time, a Romantic etude perhaps, or a variation
on a Neoclassical theme, an homage to a past that now is mine, my
mother's voice a music teacher's slow tick-tocking lesson on pacing and
interpretation, one then another turning into sound, lesson and memory
turning into sound and meaning nothing more than that, nothing more
than sound. I close the lid, the notes more than I can bear.

Section 4.

The Day After Halloween

Blustery as hell. Took my dog for a walk and leaves were scrambling like people in a disaster movie, hundreds of them, some slamming into her as if they didn't see her there. They're fleeing a giant monster stepping on them—that would be me—or a spaceship I'm imagining in the sky threatening to zap them into ashes. A panicky world we live in when dead autumn leaves can't just walk around like normal people. This is all in my head, of course, my psychology. Everything is psychology these days. We've been yearning for something real, anything, for hundreds of years now. Will we ever stop mourning the old ghosts? I'm seeing their effigies all across the neighborhood this morning, little white-sheeted figures hanging from porch eaves or propped up on fence posts, alongside black crepe paper tarantulas the size of full-grown hogs dangling from porch ceilings and pumpkins like guillotine victims flashing gruesome grins, happy to have lain their heavy burdens down, I suppose. Even the grieving is a delusion, a trick we play on ourselves to keep the myths alive, when what we're really grieving is the loss of something to grieve. We want the familiar, a gray-bearded man, dog, goat, it doesn't matter, whatever can sit or dance around a fire and then die so we can feel sad about it. But all we can do is construct sand castles in our heads, then walk around in them like Hamlet, our stockings torn, hair disheveled, no deodorant for weeks, open books upside down in our hands, our eyes, oh our eyes like balls of clay we've shaped to fill our empty sockets. We tilt our heads to the clouds as if we're seeing them. And still, blind as we are, we think we know what can save us: an open grave to jump into, the corpse in it someone we'd forgotten we loved, someone young and lovely. We'd take it in our arms and disavow any and all passions but this one, this one passion for someone we once kissed and made love to, someone we think deserves our grief.

Noodling

Little carps of meaning we can sometimes catch, with our clever hooks, sinkers, and floats, small meals such as Cumulonimbus and Pleistocene. Sometimes larger, like relativity and evolution. But the meaty fish of transcendence? Not a chance. It's a big catfish we'd like to capture and hold onto, but it's not biting and even if we had it in our hands it's too slippery. But I knew a man who could nab them that way. He'd pack up his gear after work and head out. His name was Raymond. The work was hard, lots of digging in the heat, cramped areas, crescent wrench work in narrow ditches. I once smashed a finger against a pipe bearing down on a 36-inch wrench and Raymond drove me to a doctor who, to release the pressure from the swelling, burned a hole through my nail with the end of a paper clip he'd held over a lit match. I only worked that job in the summers, the hot summers of Oklahoma, southern and western Kansas, and occasionally the Colorado mountains, but usually the hot flat lowlands of Oklahoma. Not much transcendence in the ditches there, your shirt soaked with sweat, the smell of gasoline all around you. Raymond didn't like to work hard. He had a way of disappearing when there was digging to do, but he was our foreman so we couldn't say much. He was thin and had a full head of jet-black hair like Elvis and he'd suddenly reappear after the digging, his hair slicked back and shirt tucked in like he'd just taken a crap. And he smoked a lot. It gave him an excuse to get away from the gasoline in the ditches and we'd often catch him, someone would, behind the truck or a nearby building smoking. His hands shook a lot too—we suspected he was an alcoholic. But he was nice enough, and we were in awe of his noodling, his willingness to get chest high in the Washita River and reach under rocks for big fish. He'd buy six-packs of beer for himself after work and go stick his hands into the dark unknown.

First Snow

Lifted my bedroom blinds this morning to see the first snowfall of the season, just a dusting but it's noon now and it's still coming down. We drove home from a Steve Reich concert last night through swirling wet sleet that quickly melted and gave way to more of the same, the way Reich's chords had entered and exited the stage like ghostly characters. This morning the ground was white, which seemed fitting—the Reich had stuck in our heads. From my bedroom window I could see through the light snow the leaves I raked to the curb the other day where city workers will vacuum them with a big hose, as if the leaves are water and their truck a big thirsty elephant. I raked up piles that day on the side of the house and in the back too, but was worn out by then and left them there. I noticed outside my window yesterday children playing in them and scattering them like little dust devils. In the days after raking I picked a couple of ticks off myself—one on the inside of my left thigh and another on my back—and I hoped the children's parents would be checking them that night. They lurk in the leaves I'm told, and when you find them on you bloated with your blood they can make you cringe. But they can also remind you how attractive you are, which can boost your self-esteem. Who else would stay attached to you that long? Prostitutes maybe, but they get paid for it. I heard the children outside and was pleased the leaves were a source of fun for them. Not sand on a beach, but still fun—I could hear them laughing. I wondered what it was like to laugh again jumping into a pile of leaves. The snow outside is swirling more now, flakes still small but coming down thicker and the wind's stronger than before. Even if most of the leaves on my silver maples are down, hundreds still cling to the branches—they're golden with a slight hint of green still but turning brown, and on a cloudy day like today the colors are vibrant.

Thirsting

It's a dark gray day today, warm in late November and a little wet, but mostly just dark gray. I'm remembering a dream from the other night in which I was looking out across a bay, San Francisco toward Oakland or across the English Channel from France—in the dream I wasn't sure which—and sensing an urgency to cross it, to swim it, knowing I would drown long before I reached the other side. I keep thinking of a word a friend of mine used a while back while sitting around a makeshift fire in my back yard. I told him I like to pee in my back yard at night, in the dark, and he said, "micturate"? I said I didn't know that word but when he defined it I remembered I had learned it from Faulkner and wondered why I had forgotten it. Maybe because it's too much of a mouthful for freedom, control. There's not a trace of green or yellow in the leaves on the silver maples in my yard now, past the mid-November mark, as opposed to just a few days ago when they were shining yellow and green, all lit up like big pretty candles in a dark room. I was in a bookstore earlier today and in the middle of browsing through a stack I stopped, put the book down, walked out and drove home. It had occurred to me suddenly that I was thirsting for something again when all the drink I could drink was at home, where my dog and the house's quiet tranquility awaited me.

Acknowledgements

The Antigonish Review: "Fairgrounds" "Nazi Helmet"
Arroyo: "Bats"
The Fiddlehead: "Memory"
Nimrod International: "Not Yet" "Dream"
The Pedestal Magazine: "Ars Poetica"
Sentence: A Journal of Prose Poetics: "Ghosts"

CPSIA information can be obtained
at www.ICGtesting.com
Printed in the USA
FFOW05n1453020414

9 781600 479427